INSIDE IDAHO

Photograph of Mt. Church by the author.

inside idaho
Poems, 1996–2007

Charles Potts

WEST END PRESS

The editors and publishers of the following periodicals, anthologies and book are gratefully thanked for the first publication of certain of these poems.

Rick Ardinger, *Limberlost Anthology*, Limberlost Press, Boise, Idaho
Von Binuia, *American Jones Building & Maintenance*, Seattle, Washington
Anita Boyle, Egress Studio Press Broadside, Bellingham, Washington
Matt Briggs, *Jack Straw Writer's Anthology 2007*, Seattle, Washington
Keith Browning, *Connections*, Lewiston, Idaho
John C. Dofflemyer, *Dry Crik Review*, Lemon Cove, California
Judith Roche, *Bumbershoot* Poster Poem Project, Seattle, Washington
Ford Swetnam, *Rendezvous*, Idaho State University, Pocatello, Idaho
Stephen Thomas, *Point No Point*, Seattle, Washington
Klyd Watkins, thetimegarden.com, Nashville, Tennessee
The Climbing Art, Denver, Colorado

BOOK
Jim Bodeen, Blue Begonia Press, *Lost River Mountain*, Yakima, Washington

Inside Idaho

Printed in the United States of America.
First printing: October 2009.

ISBN 978-0-9816693-4-2

Typography and design by Nancy Woodard.
Cover photo of Leatherman Pass by the author.
Author photo by Jack Large.

WEST END PRESS　•　PO BOX 27334　•　ALBUQUERQUE, NM 87125

Contents

from 100 Years in Idaho

Starlight on the Trail

Packing in the primitive
Idaho Chamberlain Basin area south
Of the main Salmon River 20 years ago
I found myself in Moose Meadows at dark
Twelve miles from the cabin
On a trail I'd been on exactly once,

Stumbling through the moonless dark
With eight pack horses, two mules,
Four extra saddle horses and one
Plumb green kid from Michigan.

I shut my eyes and sighed once,
Amazed to open my eyes and see
The trail a trifle more clearly.

I rode three steps with my eyes closed
And three with them open,
Picked up enough
Starlight on the trail
To find our dark way home.

The Homestead Act

For years my sleep was tormented with dreams
Of returning to the sided log cabin I grew up in
And finding it empty, which was no dream
But the actual condition of returning each day
From high school to be alone with the dwindling livestock
And the universal daydream of running away or leaving home.

I returned to the barnyard many years later
With my four-year-old daughter Emily in my arms
To stare at the space where the barn had been
Sawed up and shipped for its weatherbeaten pine
To yuppie ranchettes in the greater LA Basin
And all I could feel was love.

I'd expected to be able to make sense of my life
If not then, then now, if not now then when
Strolling down September lanes with tears in my eyes
Past the place where my family's cabin burned
To the ground and I heard my brother Stan describe
In the eulogy how Dad threw milk on the
Sod-roofed logs aflame and they lived the rest of that
Depression summer in a tent with a bed and a stove.

The Burnett ditch where I frequently went
As if I didn't have solitude to burn
Was a hundred yards away and of no use to anybody
Trying to put out a fire.

No one could have guessed all the "hell and high water"
I would go through in the ensuing 30 years
Except perhaps Ogden Nash and his beautiful warm note
"Everybody knows the trouble I've seen."

I remember Idaho from some preposterous angles
With the good sense to leave out the private parts,
Unlike the other log cabin that Grandpa Herb built near
Darlington with 1896 excised in the header
Still standing as a loafing shed with no foundation,
Or the Teppenyaki banquet after Dad's memorial service
Where everyone went fishing for flipped shrimp in the air.

But mostly I stick with "down the lane" to the North
Where I last walked that day with Emily
And my memories of how thin soiled, cold weathered,
High altitude, high latitude, high interest ranching
Came crashing down a no love for Lincoln lane.

Poetry on Horseback

June, 1956

Deep night,
Moonlight,
Big Lost River
Flood water,
Over the road,
Back from Houston,
Horse hooves,
Chip the crystal
Moonlit drops
Of water up,
Out in front of,
The horse and rider's
Shadow.

Raspberry

My mother was born on Bastille Day
The year the Wright Brothers finally flew
Their bike with wings over Kitty Hawk
While Henry Ford assembled his line of
Model T's
In any color you want so long as it's
Black.

Changes in the external world
Too numerous to catalog
Much less care about
Our peculiar mechanical ineptitude
For the things we've come to prefer over
People.

TV, computers, cat scanners,
Artificial hearts for millionaire
Dentists
And any number of less vital organs
Transplanted from body to body
By well-heeled doctors manipulating death
In the so-called health care delivery
System.

I love you Mom and all the wonderful
Moves you made for me beyond the obvious
Rocking
Me to sleep in your womb.

I remember raspberries
Where you taught me how to care for them
At altitudes in Idaho
Where none but the native
Bramble fruit dare grow.

On Saturday at Pioneer Park
The 4th of July leaves of the sycamore,
Otherwise rooted to the spot,
As I stare up through their canopy,
Walk into the sky.
At the end of many branches
Out from under the upside down
Crotch of the semi-barkless tree
The leaves at maximum extension say,
"This is as far as we go."

Six weeks later on my birthday
Which I have reasons to believe
You recall more vividly than your own
Judy and Emily and I picked a few
Gallons of huckleberries
On the road to Jubilee Lake
Made large by the late spring rains
Turned ripe in the Blue Mountain sun.

I turn back with tears in my eyes
Where other men fail to keep the spark
Of love at home alive to face the music of
My mother, wife, and daughter.

There is no road to be on
That can tell us more or make us feel
Better.

I'd like for you
To have my love
Not one last time
But always as you sail
From your body sick with age and medicine
Into the unknown.
Relax
And let peace be on your side
As I am by your side
500 miles away.

I'm up early on Labor Day
To run my two miles into shape
With tears streaming down my face
You will always be with me.

Like the raspberries bouncing
Off my face in the late morning dream
Of driving,
Road turned into snow and then to
Melting water
As two white bulls appear,
I speak to my friends
"Get my bike and wagon,"
As we ford past them
In the chilling runoff water of the stream.

Steps My Mother
with Some Reluctance Took

Mom had her left leg amputated last summer
And I think of all the steps she took
For the rest of us,
Now with some reluctance
In the phantom pain.
Even though her foot is gone, it still hurts.

She's no longer subject
To be embarrassed by my excesses,
Like coming to bail me out
Of the Butte County Jail
Some cold Sunday morning in October
For being
Drunker than the law allows
A 16 year-old to be
All that he is cracked up to be.

Going Blind

I never thought I'd need glasses.
I thought they were for other men,
With weaker eyes than mine.

My daughters are leading me,
To orient Emily at WA High,
To change a diaper on Natalie,
To read the letters and write the checks,
To Johanna at the University of Utah.

I lean on Lear,
Waist deep in the good earth,
Where my sanity and flowers
In often open hands are clutched.

Three daughters, each by a separate mother,
As bad as the Brazilian gubernatorial candidate,
Of whom his enemies sneered:
Vote for Minestrohne; he could be your father.
He won. I am. Here a rather more extended family
Than would fit on a right wing platform thrives.

Presbyopic but hardly blind yet
I see the world through a rigid lens
Where the fine print and the details blur,
The distinctions between sight and vision
And I just can't see waiting
For the light to leave the system,
Intact and without me.

The Joyful Lightness of Natalie

My youngest daughter just turned six,
A strong little girl going hand over hand
On the monkey bars and hanging by her knees from the
Jungle gym at Sharpstein elementary.

The welcome bump bump of the long overdue
Fall rain falling on the tin roof outside my bedroom window
Woke me in the dark where my thoughts were led
By the nightlight on in her room to her.

I don't carry her around that much anymore
Though I recall her on my back as we descended Kari Kuni Dake,
The highest volcanic cone on Kirishima plateau
After she'd climbed all but 50 feet at age 5 to the top.

Going up the 20 stairs from the main floor to the bedroom level
Of our house with her arms around my neck,
With each step I sink a little deeper into the good earth
Where children play, where the tiny fronds of ferns unfurl,
Where raindrops slide down the green stems of wheat.

How far this DNA has actually come I cannot say
Much more than to acknowledge the form it's in right now and
Rattle off some of the names it's gone under in the last
14 generations on North America:
Caldwell, Cunningham, Jones, Likes, Lewis, and Cassandra LeSueur.

Right now I know I'm queasy and content to say
I'm just a phase that life went thru
Between my mother and my daughters.

I shudder at the good times as they fell and
Fall again upon me.
Such are the hopeless minutiae of choices
Like the steady risk of being misunderstood,
I open my mouth once more in awe
Of the bright light behind the eyes of my children.

from LOST RIVER MOUNTAIN

Hide

I am a boy again,
Riding shotgun in a black and red
1948 Dodge pickup with my dad,
Crossing the Arco desert
With our cargo of cured hides.

My father was a government trapper
And I'm a government trapper's son.
Halfway to the hidehouse on
Yellowstone Avenue in Idaho Falls,
We plow through an Atomic Energy Commission plot.

The mink, the muskrat and the coyotes,
To say nothing of the beaver,
Have turned themselves inside out
Into Levi's I might get to wear,
Clean new clothes to school
With the animals under my skin.

To Idaho

Idaho is an intransigent verb.
In its infinitive form
To Idaho.

I Idaho,
You Idaho,
He, she or it Idahoes.

In the past perfect tense
I have Idahoed before.

In the future indicative
I will Idaho again.

In the pluperfect subjunctive
No one would have ever been Idahoing
If they could have thought of something better to do.

Back to Idaho

When I go back to Idaho I drive down
Through a dozen distinct strata of velveteen basalt,
Igneous layers of fired rock,
Duplicitous layers of meaning,
Ziggurating the dammed and undamned
Snake River canyon,
Trying to get underneath the bottom of things,
The source waters of the Snake
Making elaborate pictures in my limbic node
The length and breadth of the state.

The rattlesnakes come out to greet the sun
In late spring and early fall,
Basking in the canyon light
By Buffalo Eddy
Where the paleo-American artists carved the horns
Of the sheep they ate,
Petroglyphing their representations
Into the handy rock by the river's edge.

During the wet years before the climate changed
The entire Great Basin used to drain from Lake Bonneville
Over Red Rock Pass through Idaho and
On through Hell's Canyon to the Pacific Ocean
Where the flood left gravel bars
425 feet above the level of the river now.

Where did the Big Lost River flow
Before the volcanic flood
Turned the desert into a basaltic sink?

2
A big hunk of Kinikonik Quartzite
Surfaced on the foothills of the lava plain,
Between the Big and Little Lost River canyons,
That was once the sandy beach
Of a shallow Jurassic sea
When salt water last lapped
These gradually diminishing shores
Now turned upside down near Arco, Idaho.

I always suspected that the sea was upside down
In Arco, Idaho,
Home of my first real girl friends,
Gateway to the Desert and our window on the world
From my piddling perspective
On the ranch 26 miles north and west.

More than Quartzite ordinarily 700
Feet beneath the surface will be exposed.

Here in July, 1959, the police arrested us for drinking
Happier than the law allows.
Patsy and Naomi were not drunk;
They were beautiful and undoubtedly are beautiful still.

I was soon one transgression away
From being sent to Saint Anthony and
Idaho's Reform School for lost boys.

I could always use reforming.
In fact I now reform myself
Continuously and at will.

If my old friends ever think at all of me
I wonder what difference any of it makes?
Across forty years of weird weather
The children of the desert
Look back into
One another's eyes.

The Phantom Antler Mountains

Red Alert!
There is a mountain range missing in Idaho,
According to the geologists Alt and Hyndman.

Parts of it show up in
Nevada, California, British Columbia.
Could it be in southeast Oregon
Buried under cubic miles of
Basalt and ash.
Maybe it rocks on
In the mountains north of Carey.

When continent collided with the ocean floor,
The elusive Antler Mountain orogenic evidence
Was gradually destroyed by the Rocky Mountains.
Hard to lose a range of mountains
Just like that,
300 million years before Lewis and Clark.

Tramping around Idaho's mountains,
The Sawtooths and the Selkirks,
The Lost River and White Knob mountains,
You just know there just has to be more to it
Than meets the eye.

Under the earth somewhere
Else beneath the sea,
Molten lava mountains
Cooking up or melting slowly down
Going begging to be climbed are
The Phantom Antler Mountains.

Idaho Skies

Our next door neighbors to the north and east
Must bake freeze or bask
Under the big sky reputation of Montana.

Here the skies are stapled on the horizon
To the corners of your eyes
By the fixed and pitiless gaze of the raptor.

Eat me, the jackrabbit screams
In daily trial and error to be motionless
Beneath a cloudburst sky.

Cruel conservative ignorance is forcing
Its fascist predilection for a static solution
On mammals and leftover flying reptiles alike.

The lava flows have cooled and dried
The Missouri wagon wheel trails
Rutted out to Oregon.

Left behind, left over, left out,
The blue sky passes quickly over Idaho
Leaving the dark to roar

There is nothing here
Between you and
The flamboyant stars.

Stinging Nettles

I want to get a feel for the earth.
Nothing fancy
Just that strange sensation of sinking
A little farther in with each succeeding step
Backward through my spent youth and childhood.

On that lane with the nettles nearly closing it,
Dark green from a droughthy summer
Growing up out from under the unplaned plank fence
Could grab and burn you in the unsettled dust
But you kept running like you had forever to run out of time in.

So beautiful and always
My mother there between us.
If she'd disappeared for even 30 seconds
It would have happened natural
In a mutual god-numbed rut.

There is no way to make this sound
Any more horrible than it was:
Innocent desire thwarted by too much supervision
Turns paradise to ashes even memory
Cannot and will not redeem.

A Walk on the End of the World

Geyser Basin, Yellowstone Park, July 7, 1998

When the Yellowstone volcano blows again
And ashfall fills the northern hemisphere with darkness,
It is good that you can hear Chinese,
German, Japanese and French
On the trails to the fumaroles
Because it will be an international event
Off any scale of magnitude known to man or women.

When the Yellowstone volcano blows again
Practically astraddle the 45th parallel of latitude,
Which is to say halfway or equidistant
Between the North Pole and the Equator,
You'll watch the black band of darkness circle the sky
Until the lights go out on the weather channel
And the deep freeze begins.

When the Yellowstone volcano blows again
Much that doesn't freeze immediately
Will be invited to the famine,
Crops will fail in the field
As the distribution system delivers
Carnage and terror on a scale wider
Than a TV or movie camera lens.

Eagle Out

Passing near Clyde in Little Lost
Where my mother wept and worked to teach
All eight grades in a one room school house,
Two golden eagles a mile apart,
One on the roof beam of a barn,
The other on the cross arm of a light pole,
Ignore my grand noisy motion in their panoramic eyes.
The Toyota Tacoma is too big and inedible to bother with.

That was June. Fastback to March
When I was curving down the Lochsa,
A golden eagle lifted out of the righthand barpit ahead and
Flew straight toward me.
The sixty mile an hour speed of the pickup
Combined with the eagle's acceleration
Condensed the distance separating us.
I ducked at the moment of collision avoidance.

The eagles carry a message of contempt
For poets and people in their tin cans
Knocked out by their macadam.
They hold the future in their taloned claws
To rip other animals apart with their beaks
And would us too if they could reach the fleshy parts.

The Pass at Doublespring

(A Milarepan Romp)

1.

There is a region of the heart where the damned remember and go on dreaming.
In the season of outraged drainage, the whole Northwest,
No more a province than France was a province of Rome in Provençal
The singing went on underneath the slaughter.

Where in St. Anthony, Henry's Fork, the patron saint of all that's lost including causes
Gets off its river rocks over the falls in Keefer's Park,
Wherefore upstream it bubbles artesian
From the good earth squeezed between contrary pressures.

I knew and have known there'd come a time
When all my masters would be dead or mute,
So masterless agonize at misunderstanding and calm myself
On the horizon over which, through which and into which, the only future comes.

See then in the passes' bidirectionality an evenhandedness
Neither coming nor going but are
Sloped above the earthquake scarp repeatedly raising Mt. Borah
On the west through the clouds towards my love of Pahsimeroi.

2.

My love of Pahsimeroi is unbearable and runs
Strictly as water with gravity pulling it down the Canyon of Doublespring and
Onto the grave of my great grandmother Cora
Whose heart was stopped by pneumonia in 1932 at 75.

Side by side with great grandpa Robert, killed by cancer in '36,
Cora was pulled by her *corazón*
Off of the fertile soil of Iowa eroded on to Utah and
Ultimately to Goldberg to the upper river bottom of the Pahsimeroi valley.

I weep on the white stones for a ranch life lived with cattle and gone
Before I was born to the many to whom my life is owed if to anyone
Whose dreams, whose children, whose love is now
Resident in and protected by the beautiful indifferent mountains.

Cora and Robert's daughter Cecil, my great aunt in more ways than one
Who lived to be a hundred from 1890 until 1990 is here also
Alongside her 15 year old son Loy and Uncle Chris,
The Carlsons my kin, their *kine*, my kind, my folk, my family.

3.
My family in the mountains of silence connected by unpaved roads
Over Doublespring from Pahsimeroi to Big Lost River
Or Southeast to Little Lost and back over Pass Creek towards Darlington
Defining the crooked county line between Butte and Custer counties.

We share a line, we share a time, we share the Lost River Mountains
With big time beyond our rockheaded geologic comprehension as if
They've always been here as we see them now
We know better and are unconsoled.

I'm going back to Upper Pahsimeroi beyond Horse Heaven
To the high country meadows where the staggering ziggurat of Mt. Borah
Penetrates the thinning sky. Everything in the desert is so green this spring,
As if God was the weather and could change our *El Niño* minds.

Step by step, rock by pebble, sagebrush in topsoil moistened by rain,
I'll get to the top of these mountains and the bottom of this process
If it kills me as it kills me before it kills me,
I feel like letting the lightning-like strike of consciousness discharge.

Pahsimeroi Eki

Pahsimeroi Eki begins to take shape
In imaginary union spliced between
Shoshoni and Nihongo.
Formerly there was no Eki in Pahsimeroi.
This is the way to the Pahsimeroi station.

The Eki Kanji has its parts
Contributing to the union.
It is a horse up against a flute,
A shaku hatchi in fact,
A call for transportation.

A left handed horse with binocular vision
A right handed flute with erotic overtones
Playing its tune in the great outdoors
Beyond the Granger's Hall in May
In a Uto-Aztecan desert.

While only the station is stationary,
Everything else takes on the character of constant change.
The station is molecular morphemes traveling
In stationary formation
Composing Pahsimeroi Eki.

Pahsimeroi's a river by definition
With a single grove of trees.
Pahsimeroi's a valley of the union
Between horses and music.
Pahsimeroi Eki's where we hear
How the West was lost
In the gasp where the world begins.

My father used to whistle for his horses.
The bright ones came galloping at the sound.
He had no flute but horseback transportation
To escape from English into sound.

I need to get out of here.
Can you call me a horse.

You're a horse, Pahsimeroi Eki.
We've been stalled at the station
For a long time.

The Auction Block

Hardly a month went by
In those long, bitterly cold winters
Between the end of the Korean War
And 1961 when I escaped to Pocatello
In the Big Lost River Valley of collusion
That I didn't accompany my father
To a farm auction.

The banks are still standing while the people crack and cry.
Feel the heat from the fires of scrap wood rising,
Smell the coffee, see the steam, from hot breath in the air,
Going up with the glisten of snow chilling everything,
The way steel on frozen machinery gleams below zero,
Waiting to freeze your tongue to the fire.

I learned to think of the farms we were going to
As the scenes of failure which they certainly were
Albeit of a vastly more complicated kind
Than I ever dreamed I was witnessing.

At the end of the parade of the fucked-up Fifties
When my own parent's auction took place,
I was too embarrassed to attend.
You know how a parent can embarrass a teenager
Just by walking into a room?
I remember them now awkwardly trying to keep pace
In a macabre dance of marriage and microeconomics,
All the shouting, finger pointing, misplaced blame,
Lost dreams and botched opportunities for sale.

What could they have felt like finally to see
Their furniture, their livestock, their land and their lives
Available to the highest bidder?
Relief at the belief that it was finally over?
Anger at each other for who else was handy to blame?
Fear of the future in circumstances potentially even grimmer?
Even a drunken rock and roll basketball player can't bear
To see his fidgeting parents destroyed.

Immanuel Kant should have come here
In his relentless quest for dignity.
I was gone in white Luskys to a basketball game
Having finally made the team.
Later that spring my horses were auctioned
To salvage a nest egg for my college education.
Eventually all but the most meticulous
Managers were forced out of business in similar ways.

Only a complete audit of the banking system's
Hidden cadres of superficial beneficiaries,
Stock holders and speculators strung up through time,
Would complete the signs of evil in a tux and tie.

The season is too short, the odds unmercifully long
For all but the most heroic couples and
Their 16 hour a day value-added cooperation
Could make work for many are still on the land
Because of Chapter 12 bankruptcies and
Suits that wouldn't have the faintest idea
What real work consists of.

from LOST RIVER MOUNTAIN

Mom and Dad

I was raised in a desert by a father who
Believed I was someone else's child
And a mother's conditional love.

My mother had brains
And my father had guts.
When I'm good I'm using both.

My mother was very sociable.
My father did ten thousand things alone.

My mother loved to spend money.
My father wanted to invest.
I've invested all of our money
So there will be more to spend.

My mother wanted to have a good time.
My father wanted to survive.
I survive by having a good time.

I'm the predictable result of
The underlying structure of my life.

Coming to Terms

Coming to terms
Terms of endearment
Terms of agreement
Terms of reconciliation
With my father
Since there were none
With my mother
Anymore
Now that they are both dead
Dad reduced to ashes
Mom to a one-legged cripple.

Not that operating
Three diversified and non-contiguous
Ranches, farms and pasturage
While teaching school and trapping
As they raised four kids
Through one Great Depression
Three wars where one was wounded
The consolidation of the school system
The Eisenhower high interest 50s
With a banker in their hip pockets
Wouldn't have been enough of
An eighteen to twenty hour a day nightmare
Not counting dreams
They had apparently to have
Their minuscule operation in global terms
Audited by the IRS.

Terms of the audit
Testing whether or not
The gain on the sale of that cow,
The depreciation on that piece of
Over-priced machinery,
Was properly accounted for
Calculated and reported
Adding bookkeeping to
The ten thousand tasks of Hercules
That diversified agriculture was
Before they and 50 million others
Were forced off of the land as
Non-economic nuisances and debris
To fill one day the
Malls of America
With their hungry eyes and dreams.

Terms of understanding
Terms of disbelief
School terms starting and stopping
Living on Rainbow Trout and Dolly Varden
Venison backstrap and the occasional
Sacrificial lamb from their modest flock
Selling milk to the creamery in
Exchange for butter
After the churn had stopped churning
The separator spinning
The lighter cream from the heavier milk
A beef here
Chicken every day after the flock of
Day old baby chicks
That had arrived in cardboard boxes on
The Union Pacific spur line matured,
Boxes of a hundred divided up in quarters to be kept warm
Under heat lamps in a chicken coop
I now notice when I pass
What we used to call our place
Is tilting gradually into the gently sloping ravine.

Add guiding and election watching
Taking in the family strays
Sending money over the phone
Building a potato cellar
Covering it with Bentonite
To cash in on the boom and bust of
Idaho's famous
To the things they did to try
To stave off failure
And the picture begins to complete itself.

The terms of the failure of their farming operation
The terms of the divorce making official
The terms of the failure of their marriage of over 30 years.
The beautiful night I remember when
Stan & Joy threw a party for them
At the ranch house on Alder Creek
When they were still friends with the
Émigrés from Pasadena
The silver anniversary of their wedding in 1932.

How can I
Why have I
Not come to terms
With all or any of this before
As the ordinary people watch us walk
Into another Great Depression
With the same distracted speculators
Looking for a cheap profit
To which they added no value but
The cash they took from poor people
The defenseless land, the indifferent sea.

The Old Pioneer Cemetery

1.

There are 47 graves ID'ed with headstones or markers
In the Old Pioneer Cemetery on the east bench between
Darlington and Moore in the Big Lost River Valley and
30 of them are members of my family,
10 of them children who died when
The infant mortality rate was ratcheting off the chart.

So what does that make me,
The keeper of the dead
For my generation?
And in that regard I most resemble this
50 square yards of the good earth.

The topsoil is so thin on this alluvial fan
I could scrape it away with my hand.
Only cheat grass and crested brome
Turn green here in season underneath the
Sagebrush as the white clouds
Collide with King Mountain.

My sister and I tore three tumbleweeds
From the subsoil newly turned
Over our mother's grave,
The last of the Gray line on this tour of family lineage.

The Big Lost River Valley is disconnected
From the rest of the known and unknown world,
Although the entire globe is beginning to resemble
Gray's "Elegy Written In A Country 'Grave'yard,"
By mountain passes, lava flows, volcanic plains,
Earthquakes, Sun Valley and the radioactive Arco desert.

I weep like a child among our children's graves.
The graves of my Grandmothers and Grandfathers,
Who raised me to be strong on scar tissue,
Get me up off my bended knees
To fix my genetic makeup.

I do dead reckoning
Without reference to the fixed or shooting stars,
Grinning with the guts of
The man who cracked the code
Of the criminally conservative west.

2.
The people buried in the Old Pioneer Cemetery
Have grown up out of the ground into my feet.
I no longer walk alone and I've outgrown
The nervous need for individualism as I become
The firm voice from the branches of this extending family tree.

For more than one hundred years our people
Have been weeping into this alluvial mud.
Look both ways between the tears at how we were
Torn like the reluctant teeth of wisdom one by one
From the land and flung into tiny towns and cities.

We are nearly a mile above sea level in the
Big Lost River Valley of collusion between the bankers
And the idle rich elsewhere who demanded as if it were their right
To overcharge us for the time value of money,
Which has been going down all the time.

While the interest rates conversely have gone up.
Usury is impolite; as a term, it is intended to beggar the imagination.
I feel terrible at the death of my brother Don.
Dottie hands the American Flag the American Legion
Has just consecrated his All-American grave with off to me.

I accept the folded cloth of fear
The other old Vets' eyes were filled with.
Death will soon space them all out
Beyond the battlefields and warships,
Beyond further redemption by dignified survivors.

The lid is down on Don's coffin, the Old Glory folded.
The twisted barbed wire and lariat wreath
Is in my sister's hands.
The next *Lexington* Reunion will have to celebrate without him.
I tore up the invitation at his instigation.

I go back to celebrate our old times and
The grace with which he danced the western swing in
Cowboy boots, having held on to his loafers so that
The coral reefs he was shipwrecked on on Tongatabu
After the Battle of the Coral Sea
Could not cut his feet.

Raspberry Redux

Now that the women I learned the most
About raspberries, hard work and love from,
My mother and Dorothy Ivie, are both dead,
I pull the rapidly growing morning glory
From the bases of my transplanted canes
After all the other work is done
And the late afternoon spring sun
Warms the earth and my back,
Slightly bent, as gloved hands grip
The handle of a hoe
With a thin, intentional blade.

Lullaby of the Lochsa

Hide the Mountain

Traveling through crumpled mountains
On highway 20 in central Idaho
Between Hill City and Mountain Home,
I read the book of rock* from shotgun
Extolling the differences
Between granite and basalt
To Natalie in the backseat
Who as a 4th grader gets to study
Earth science
While her mother drives.

Natalie listens patiently and with interest
To paragraph after paragraph
From her well intended parents.

Near the crest of the summit
On Castle Rock in Goodale's Cutoff
Elevation 5527 feet, she leans over the seat to say,
"If this were flat it would be pointless."

*Alt and Hyndman's *Roadside Geology of Idaho*

Pilgrimage to Pahsimeroi

The slate at the gate to Pahsimeroi
Where the mouth of the river merges
Into the Salmon at Ellis
Crooked woven pole fences
Keep the range unopened.

Pacific Power has a hatchery in the mouth of the Pahsimeroi.
Ahead of me the Lost River Mountains have a dust of snow.
Angus cattle in the pastures
Deep in the brown grass of November
Did I see a longhorn? Tiny Texans
Little cattle; big horns.
I admire the conical peaks
At the head of little Morgan Creek
Having a bout of log cabin fever
I can see May over to my right
The cemetery and the pine tree in it.
I'm back in Pahsimeroi again.

Double Duty on Doublespring Pass

Stopping to take a
Piss on the pass
I remember Hideyoshi Toyotomi and Tokugawa Iseyau
Eight years before the battle of Sekigahara
When they'd decided how to divvy up Japan
Taking a piss on the pass to cement the deal
And are known to this day among Tokyo schoolboys as
The two pissers on the Kanto Plain.

Thanks to them you can still piss practically anywhere in Japan
Including the main streets of Otemache and Marunouchi
As proof if you need it
That men have bigger needs than decorum
Except after Christianity bombed out in Nagasaki
Corrupting urine as thoroughly as flesh.

Double duty on Doublespring.
I'm a poet not a general leader of men.
The pass doesn't exist for our purposes.
It's only a low spot on the upthrust
Beckoning a road because lift is expensive
Where the laws of the conservation of energy
Apply to every thing alive.

So I piss on the pass below timberline
To give up the heat in exchange for relieving
The pressure on my bladder.
There is something disarmingly simple about
The smell of moist sagebrush suspended
In 8300 feet of thin air.

The New Moon

"There's a new moon, over my shoulder
And an old log in my heart."

Is the way I used to sing
My parent's favorite song
Driving them slightly nuts,
Misunderstanding
Old "love" in my heart
For something beautiful that lay on the ground,
I could walk on and understand.

Stanley told me how our wagoneering ancestors
Came down Doublespring Pass from Pahsimeroi
Towing a log for brakes
To keep a loaded wagon from overrunning a team.

"There's a new moon, over my shoulder
And an old log in my heart."

Pioneer Cemetery, 7:00 PM

September 15, 2001

It's very peaceful tonight in Lost River Valley.
The sky is almost closed with clouds.
The sun shines through a few over Antelope Valley
While a half dozen nylon insect hang gliders sail
In the launch site breeze behind me on King Mountain.

I'm sitting on my grandmother's tombstone
Looking west toward White Knob.
I can hear somebody plinking
Shots at something toward the southeast.

I noticed my great grandfather Henry Morgan Evans
Was born on September 11, 1854,
147 years to the day before 9/11.
How close the past all seems right now.

Walter Evans, one of Aunt Stella's children
Was born on the 10th and died on the 11th of September, 1917.
She lost her twins, Mary and Martha,
Born and died on the same day, October 28, 1907.

I took a picture of her now abandoned cabin on the way by,
The cabin where we had the wake for her husband Uncle Lou
In 1949.

It's only been four days since 9/11.
The asymmetrical war talk in video fascism is way out of hand.
It's raining briefly on Mackay now
Dehydrated by a long and persistent drought.

I think I'll split before the plinkers
Misfire with an ironic ricochet and kill me
In our own cemetery yet.

Lullaby of the Lochsa

Weippe Prairie
6 dead deer; one blue heron
What beautiful light and trees
10 miles south of Orofino
5 Mile Creek
To go with Four Mile Creek in Washington
I had a lot to walk about
I discovered my life was an example of
Redemption through survival
Lots of things have happened to me
I've caused a lot of things to happen

2 years ago I went over the top
Beautiful slow twisting drive
From Kamiah to Lewiston
Just south of the bridge where
The Indian ex-cons picked us up in 1961
Who owns the river?

Just past a sign for Looking Glass
What about this famous Indian Chief
Rear View Mirror
Elderberries
Sung Dynasty clouds
Hanging in the tops of pine trees
Pilgrimage to Pahsimeroi
The granite on the roadside
Slick with water
Fire Creek
Song of the Lochsa
Love Song of the Lochsa
Lochsa River Song

Split Creek
The bridge I never walked on
Halfway between
Split like you're on fire
Way up on the top
I can see snow
Lochsa beaches granite boulders
Rapid action white water photography
Horsetail Falls Creek
Shoestring Falls and Wild Horse Creek
Oh what a freshet Wild Horse Creek is
Marconi's Creek
A freshet coming down a
Groove of granite
Not more than 4 inches wide
Crossing North Idaho
Like "Crossing North Cache"
At Eagle Creek
A Sung Cloud hanging on the hiway
Hanging even heavier on the river
We make friends with and pass right through

Bathroom at Fish Creek
Sardine Creek
Lochsa Historical Ranger Station
At No See'em Creek we just cut through
Another little Cloud of Sung
More and more Sung Clouds
Mile marker 125
The light that through the Sung Cloud beams

Whoa
Bald Mountain Creek
Tamaracks picking up the light
Look like cathedral spires in the pine
Gets more drier as we get
Closer to the top
Looks like a clear cut
Aspens totally bare
Look like birch ghost trees
Along with the yellow tamarack
And the still resplendent green
Eagle Mountain
Lost Creek
No relation to Lost River
Lost Lake Lost Ocean
Stephen Thomas through the crucible
Saddle Camp Road
A whole ridge of tamarack pine
Post Office Creek
With gate locks ascension trail step off
Much mistletoe
Get it all in the same frame
It wouldn't be impossible
But it would be a very large canvas

Jerry Johnson Campground
The foot bridge at Warm Springs Creek
Squaw Creek and Squah Creek
Pines get scraggly and
There's a little water on the road
Could have been slick this morning
Papoose Creek
16 pines
Lochsa Lodge
Left the wild and scenic river
Parachute Hill
Redemption through survival
The most biologic of victories

Passion Creek
Shotgun Creek
Crooked Creek
5 hours to the top of Lolo
Half moon over my left shoulder
Montana Diorite stones
I walked that trail with Emily
That summer I went to Mackay
To bring my mother to Walla Walla
To stay with us for a while
Dolomites and diorites
A live deer
Bouncing along in the barpit
Ft. Fizzle
Must be a Lewis and Clark thing
Ricochet 24 years too late

A great set of Sawtooth Mountains
5 miles south of Hamilton
The Bitterroots
The Lost Horse Creek
Write a book called sleep
I took my nap 15 miles from
The Idaho line
Broken heart attack
Log house in log formation
2 ridges collide
Broken Arrow Café
Fine Mexican food
Great mixed metaphor
Gibbonsville, Idaho
Appaloosa mule
47 miles to North Fork
Sliding along with the ripples
At the River of No Return

Tim Waterman's friends in Puerto Vallarta
Frank Malgesini in Chihuahua
Herd of sheep 10 miles in
20 miles up
444 North side
Panther Creek Taco Buffet
Herd of sheep in the orchard
Wring our hands in unison
Establish a pace and
Eat up the miles
I'm looking down at
The Silicon Road
Owl Creek Event

If you're mistaken that will become apparent
If you're uncertain that will be apparent
Before anything gets even said

Make something as peaceful
As the Salmon River on Halloween
A man in a blue boat
With 2 golden oars

From Salmon to Changsha

Unmitigated ignorance is the human condition.
Old time red barked dogwoods thrive on
Island Park in Salmon.
Riffle—river stones
God for the washing they have taken.
Deer tracks in the dirt and sand.
The sound of water over rocks always takes me back.

Orange Island also long and skinny
More or less also in the middle of town
But big enough people live on it
The Xiang Jiang like the Salmon flowing North.
Between the river and the river is an island.
Go north to where the river comes back together.
Beaver eating itself out of house and home.
The island comes to a point and the river comes together.
No more island this way.
There's only the river and the island's underneath it.

Next morning jogging to the south end
Like I did in Changsha on Orange Island
Startling a flock of geese south off south point
Huge bunch of sideways cottonwood tree trunks
Washed into a heap when the river was high.
I can still see the moon and Venus
The Morning Star I yammer at the students
To get out of bed to see,
Get out of bed and look up.

The Salmon is much cleaner than the Xiang
But can it be kept that way?
This island town is tiny by comparison:
4 million people in Changsha; 4 thousand in Salmon maybe.
Raindrops spot the river stones.
I heard a horse I thought had a blanket on it.
It was only an appaloosa underneath an apple tree
With a bay horse for a companion.

Hopelessly Rexrothian

I look up to see the great pink bottomed clouds
Of February morning
Through the etched fleur-de-lis glass and
De Foggi's blue and yellow medicine wheel

And I think:
Why not write something hopelessly Rexrothian
Since I have been transcribing notes I recorded
Four months ago for the "Lullaby of the Lochsa."

In love with Sung misty clouds I took down
Tseng Kung's beloved "Chao-Yin Monastery" poem
And blew the dust that had settled
From the top of the book three times

Before I got it off.
How I neglect
Some of the things
I truly love

Tagore's rendition which closes
With a pang of pure music:
"I am overfond of lonely places
Where water flows and sings."

Papoose Comes back to My Dream

In my dream I'm bareback
Leading Papoose
Across a busy street
With hackamore and chain
Mounting my high school horse
My Appaloosa back
Along the roadway
Above the crumbling cliffs
With magnificent mountains
At my back and front.

We come to a locked gate
Followed by an open one.
I remove the wire latch
She jumps up the embankment
Onto the planks
The bridge across the spring fed stream
Which is our introduction
To the field
I recognize
Trees, landscapes, and an imaginary
Shangrila valley
Opens up in the middle of
My dreams, my memory,
My memory of dreams
My horses, my mountains, our extraordinary life
All fading out in dreams.

How can I ever write a poetry as beautiful
As my life with horses and mountains has been?

The Wreckage from Red Hill

For Travis Catsull and Brandon Follett

March 19. 2000

Yesterday I took Travis and Brandon
Up to Red Hill so they could see for themselves
The wreckage in the valley of the Portneuf
Through the chipped white pre-Raphaelite
Acropolis intimating pillars
Underneath the blue chamber of commerce sky
Across the Snake River Plain
Beyond the big and little buttes
The overthrust belts of the Lost River Mountains
Snowy white with limestone fragments poking through;
A heavenly city composed entirely of rock;
King Mountain, Smiley Mountain, The White Knob Mountains
How can beauty be so useless
Or does it have to be practical, any use at all?

All I betray is my own fear.
In the company of articulate youth
When the last of day-before-yesterday's snowmelt
Was lifted from the pillar tops
By the wind and dashed its slush at our feet,
We were mildly started,
Our mutual interest in possibility
Bonding us briefly in the breeze.

Freezing Rain

What looked like a drop of water
About to drip from the Burr Oak twig
Turns out as I touch it to be
A frozen drop of water
Which won't be dripping
Until the temperature goes up.

Across the yard to the west the total tops
Of the Arbor Vitae I now notice are
Filled with such frozen water drops
Giving them a sheen I've never seen before.

How lucky we are to be alive.
New stuff every day
Which we can't even imagine.

I took the dog who can't make her mind up this morning
Back outside to see the frozen rain again.

The Pine trees all have it too
And are a color that beggars a blue green description.

Nearly every twig of the bare branched Oak
Has one tiny drop at its end.

What a design to delight my heart.

I was not so happy the first time I knew freezing rain
Decades ago in December on Hiway 95
In an old Ford u-haul truck, a hysterical wife
And a six-month old baby strapped on the seat between us
Sliding towards Sandpoint.

I may camp out in the backyard this morning to watch
This water change phases.

In the front yard the drops resemble ear studs
On the pendulous rhododendron petals.

Pahsimeroi ¼ Moonlight on the Pines
July 25, 2005, 2:00 AM

If you listen to the West Fork Pahsimeroi water long enough
It becomes apparent just how noisy and indifferent
Water really is.

The north slopes of the Lost River Range
Unintentionally too made a deal
With the weather to collect this water.

Salmon navigating a force field of migration
Could find their way back up these streams
They were washed out of as fry years before
Anadromous hydro electrocution.

The night chills me awake;
At daylight I'll climb Leatherman.

SUNBURNT ROMANTIC

Sunburnt Romantic

Once I was a sunburnt romantic
With a flat stomach and a bleeding heart
Knocked out by my own idealistic daydreams
As a child laborer on a family farm
Circling the redundant unplowed field
On a tractor to nowhere
Surrounded by mountains, animals and trees
Never for a moment distrusting my destiny
While living forward to a tomorrow that never came.

As the years went by and tomorrow worsened
I drank too much and got sarcastic
With authority figures:
Parents, coaches, teachers, police, professors, preachers,
Draft boards, politicians, newspaper editors, bullies in general,
From the adolescent locker room terrorists forward
To uninformed, ill informed, misinformed, uniformed
Soldiers, bankers and bureaucrats
All dolled up in predatory aggression.

With a few friends and more drugs and evasive moves
Than I'd care to recall
We survived as cultural cripples,
The roadkill of idealism flattened out by power.

2

A father and a poet I make room for my offspring.
The way on horseback, saddle sore,
I herded sheep on sagebrush mountains:
Brought them down from the pinnacles of their blind ascent
Fished them out of criks
Untangled them from barbed wire
Hiked down miles of railroad track seeking the lost herd
Ears cocked for the tinkle of
Dangling clapper on brass bell
Pulled the wool from dead sheep's bodies
Tamped their wool into tubular bags
Soaked and hung on giant racks
Greased with organic lanolin
Crawling with sheep ticks
Drenched their wounds with creosote
To boil the white squirming maggots from the putrid flyblown flesh
Removed them from alfalfa fields
Where their two-toned stomachs and gaseous chemistry
Would have bloated them like the swarming ticks
Who got sucking mouth parts stuck and swelled up with blood
Kept them out of the mouths of coyotes
Who'd eat them alive before their hearts stopped bleating
Tucked them in at night in canvas covered sheepsheds
Beyond below zero winter January wind
Full in the morning of steamy sheep breath
Assisted them at difficult births
Cleaned the noses of the newborns
Squirted ewe's milk into naïve mouths
Nursed the bum lambs with beer bottles full of warm cow's milk
Heated on wood stoves and sucked through rubber nipples
Skinned the still born dead and slapped the hide onto the living
To fool the adoptive mother with the smell of her own grief
Trailed along behind the herd
The constituent element that kept it all together
Animal husbandry on hoof
A real shepherd of actual sheep
A weaver of patterns in wool.

3
Outside the pattern chaos theorists
Sip expensive aperitifs
Paid for by Christian legislators
Who don't know what they're doing.

Inside the pattern melody rises,
Naked as love in a pasture of gymnophobes.
Love me, eat my sheep.

Language was the first technology.
While we talk, nature recedes.
Once we got our feet underneath us
And butts big enough to walk upright and run,
We let go of the branches we used to hang out on
In fear of the deadly predators
Who once ruled the forest floor and
Now rule the endless streets.

I could see my larynx coming
On a wave of sound welling up to pour
Out of an upright throat to pound chimpanzee dreams
With the deadly gene for speech.

Sonny Boy

Sonny Boy
Registered Appaloosa stallion numero uno
Dad brought back from California
Wrapped in a horse blanket
Against the double digit below zero Idaho cold.

Sonny Boy picked me up in his teeth
When my back was turned
In the stackyard forking hay
Through the Levi jacket and shook
The ragdoll living shit out of me.

The scars of his incisors made a horseshoe shape.
I carried the sign of the stallion on my back
The rest of the way through high school.

I've been chewed up and spit out.
I know what I'm talking about.
I've been in the horse's mouth.

Spud Harvest

Admiral Hyman G. Rickover,
The father of the nuclear navy,
Plied the seas of the volcanic Idaho desert
In the fall of 1954
To look in on and congratulate himself for
The progress being made on the engine of the *Nautilus*
At the Atomic Energy Commission installations
Midway between Arco and Idaho Falls.

What he found to rave about
Beyond the isotopes and his own
Clear path to public money
To finance his private Idaho fantasies
Was most of the school districts in Eastern Idaho
On vacation for two weeks so that the children could help with
Spud harvest.

"What are you people raising here,
Children or potato pickers?"

It's a pity empires feel obliged to locate
Their most dangerous activities at greatest remove
From their population centers,
Otherwise the beautiful deserts of the American West
Would never have been radioactivated.

The droll, bib-overalled, LDS and other peasants of Eastern Idaho,
Second cousins of the earthy and grateful European peasants
Depicted in Van Gogh's "Potato Eaters,"
Have a right to wonder:
Which part of the nuclear navy is protecting them from what?

Bastille Day, July 14, 2000

Today is my mother's birthday who'd be 96 were she still alive.
I've been thinking lately of summers around our place in Idaho,
How incredibly busy everyone was, how impossibly hard everyone worked.
Were we all that deprived of the capacity to relax by what?

A typical day would start in the dark changing water.
You don't really change water; you change the setting,
Move it down the field across pastures or rows of potatoes.

After changing several streams of water there were the cows to milk,
Horses, pigs and chickens around the barnyard to feed and water.
All of this, a half day's work, before breakfast.

If it was spring, immediately after breakfast, land was prepared for planting.
Plow, disc, harrow, drill.
If midsummer as it is now, there was
Hay to mow, rake, bale, stack.

Change the water again before lunch which was usually huge:
Meat, potatoes, vegetables and bread.

On good days there might have been ten minutes after lunch to rest.
Before OSHA's laughable fifteen minute breaks twice a day.

Afternoons were like mornings in reverse.
Same hard grind out in the field.
Around the house my mother did the laundry,
Chopped the heads off chickens, scalded them and plucked their feathers,
Cleaned the house, picked raspberries, tended the garden,
Cooked three enormous meals a day.
Incidentally, she taught school for 25 years in the middle of this.

Change the water again before supper
And after which milk the cows again.
Change the water yet one more time in the desert before dark.
It was dark when we finished and dark when we started and
Dark most of the time in between.

It is why I sometimes refer to myself as a calvinist with a small "c."
Now I'm as busy as my parents used to be.
I take time to consider who and what I'm working for.
I want to rescue some small islands in my unconscious mind
To shipwreck myself upon or merely visit occasionally.
What will I be like when I liberate the country?
Liberate myself from all this dreadful work?

The Lamb in the Oven

The newborn lamb was freezing in the blizzard
In the sheep corral behind
An unplaned slab lumber plank fence.

I picked him up and ran
Down the lane toward the house
Fenced in on all sides
With him tucked under my jacket
And a big fear in my heart.

I don't want him to die.
If he dies I get yelled at
As if it were my ten-year-old fault
The ewes started lambing early
In the snow instead of the sheepshed
Where we hadn't yet started putting them
For the January night.

You have any idea how many dying animals
I've held in my arms?
Helpless hands ineffectively fumbling
For an answer to keep life from escaping,
To save the young and weak, tears and all.

Inside the kitchen on my knees I put
The frozen lamb in a cardboard box,
Leaving the door open after I shove him in
To the oven of the wood burning cook stove
To bake him back to life.

Smoke Rise

For Stan and Joy

Smoke rise
Formerly "sun" rise
An immense red sun is revealed by earth turn lifting through the
Smoke cloud completely smothering the eastern horizon
Across the Blue Mountains towards Idaho and Montana,
A disaster long before the governor declared it total.

Eleven western states have wild fires burning beyond control.
Think of my brother and his wife in their log cabin on Colson Crik,
Four miles east of where the Middle Fork runs into
The main Salmon,
The Frank Church River of No Return Wilderness on fire
Where his hunting business is also
Going up in smoke.

Last year he fell down across twenty feet of hard rock,
Broke eleven ribs, tore his shoulder up.
At 66 he still tries to
Dance across the wilderness.

I used to ride horseback across Chamberlain Basin,
A few of 3 million acres burned in two days
In the great August fire of 1910,
A few stately yellow pines on south sloping ridges
Mostly brittle little lodge poles surrounding
The Meadow of Doubt.

There is not an allegory.
The burn is on.
Smoke rise
Upwards toward the fire
Underneath the sun which allows us
To make matters worse.
Willfully and in ignorance
We watch it burn.

Milking Cows at 20 below Zero

Outside in January
Old Bob's teats warm
My hands on the inside but
The backs are frostbitten.

The wind blows around the corner of the barn
On the metal five gallon bucket I'm using
For a milk stool,
Freezing my ass to the can.

This old big boned blue roan cow
I'm milking isn't easy to milk
Even in the summer time.

It's too cold to cry.
I remember thinking scared
Is this all my life is ever going to amount to?

Harrowing

Harrows are dragged behind tractors across fields
Hydraulically or under their own weight in gravity
Breaking up clods after plowing to level the field
For seeds that grow into plants that feed us all.

Around and around or back and forth heavy disks
Lighter springtoothed and spiketoothed harrows
Raise topsoil to the level of dust and aggravation
When the wind blows it down your neck and into your teeth.

Tractors are slow, time is taken off the farmer's
Allotted skein to be burned up by children who think
Bread grows in plastic bags on supermarket shelves
Under florescent lights beyond automatic doors in air conditioned air.

Who cares for the land now that soil has been turned into
Dirt by petro-chemical agribiz as it hydroponically sprouts
Genetically altered seeds into super crops in silicate soil
With all the humus and consistency of pulverized glass.

Harrow the land, harrow the poem
Drag it back and forth in front of the audience
Until some of the teeth sink in.

The Little Russian Boy

The little Russian Boy inside
Who never had a decent pair of skates,
Danced with Dostoevsky on the dark
Ice of Idaho.

Today he takes a stand against American bullies
Whose ignorant effrontery keeps them
Rewriting Russian History
As if they'd lived it themselves,
Taking credit for killing Hitler in Europe,
When 20,000,000 Russians died
And only 250,000 Americans died
On all fronts in the disaster of World War II.

Certain famous newscasters
War babies also
Ceremoniously dubbed the Americans
Who fought in World War II
The Greatest Generation.

A colossal mistake to honor the superlative moment
Our culture passed from incipient democracy
To universal state and empire.

100 to 1,
Americans did not knock
The Berlin Wall down.

The grim reaper is gleefully recycling these WW II vets
At the alarming rate of 1,000 a day,
Subsequently rubbing out the romance of war.

Dirt Road Death

Elegy for Big Al Hansen (July 4, 1980–May 18, 1999)

The details of your death
"At about 6:05 a.m. Saturday
On the East Pass Creek Road
About 28 miles north of Howe
About four miles west of the intersection
With the Little Lost Highway at Clyde . . ."

So decorously separated
By your hometown newspaper,
The Arco Advertiser quoted above,
From the story of the services,
One at the chapel, one at the high school,
And your athletic history full of friends and lovers,
Lead me to ask what your death was really all about,

For your parents and your brother
Who now stagger through the day
Under the final weight of their loss
Only to stagger through the night
Into sleep and terrifying dreams.

I never knew you but I've been on that horny road
To survive enough drunken car wrecks
On early morning Idaho Highways forty years before
To feel some affinity. For you,
It was still Friday night.

Your fishtailing Chevy pickup
For 317 feet 6 inches
Apparently swapped ends and must have been traveling backwards
When it left the road and rolled over through the borrow pit
Three complete times before coming to a total wreck
113 feet from where it had thrown you,

Who traveled the tortured roads of Idaho,
Blessed brother, lover, son and friend.
Dirt road death made memories of you.

Listen to the Water on the Houston Bridge

If I sit on this bridge long enough
All the water on earth
Will eventually pass beneath me.

The Red Fox at Houston

1.
I went back to a place I'd once known love
    And everything'd changed
Except the sound of water.

My knees nearly buckled at the Lost River Bridge.
Through the wet willow smell tord the old swimming
Hole in my past,
Overwhelmed by memory and odor,
I staggered down the lane toward Mt. McCaleb
Seized by the sensation I was wobbling north
Across the very spot where forty years before
We screwed away our shard of time.

The old swimming hole had cottonwood logs
Under water now rocked in with quartzite riprap
To protect this abused tongue of still topsoiled land
From Lost River's relentless erosive meander.

I cried outloud with my arms flung on
To the inside top of a metal pole gate, quite clearly posted:
NO TRESSPASSING
PRIVATE PROPERTY
About what a mess I've made of my life.

2.
I considered turning west to trespass deeper
Beyond the ramshackle loading chute
Into the river bottom pastures of my dissolute youth
Still wrapped in six-stringed barbed wire geometry
To seize the hole in my past by its ragged edges
To cuddle the compass of my mangled heart
To rely on the shape of the wandering river
To bring the definition of water to life.

3.
I gave it up to turn back south
To the backlit clouds in the White Knob sky
Leaving the limestone triumph of McCaleb behind me
In its baked pink sunset afterglow.

I can't weep my life away.
I worked all day and I still have
250 miles to drive in the dark.

The red fox I disturbed striding
Drunk on gravity
In a shattering
Reverie of shame.
Why'd I never seen a red fox
In the Lost River bottom before?

4.
Crying brings the love back up
To where I killed my dog and
Not my father or myself.

I went back east on the Houston Lane
To rejoin the road I drove out on
The Lost River Valley in accelerating darkness
To remember how I heard in Seattle and mistook in Berkeley
The sound of laffing
Water for my name.

WILD HORSE

Upside Down Ocean

October 12, 2004

The sky looks like
An upside down ocean, Ann said,
The underbellies of the clouds lit up
By the falling twilight sun.

Ann knew how to take a risk.
She joined the Peace Corps.
She went to Paraguay.
She married a poet.

Wild Horse

For Ann Marie Weatherill
May 30, 2004, 4:50 AM

I drove to Wild Horse in the dark
Where you rode your bike with friends
Where reckless arrogant drivers
Can no longer kill you.

I want you to be safe and
Know that you are loved.

I'm following The Milky Way
Highly visible in the Big Lost River night
One of the reasons we keep
Coming back to Idaho
Arcing from horizon to horizon
Driving south tord Copper Basin
Silhouetted east of Antares
It disappears behind the Pioneer Mountains.

Five miles north of Hyndman Peak
Before dawn sitting down
In the middle of Wild Horse Crik
Where The Milky Way appeared to me
To reenter the earth
Opposite a gully filled with snow
Curving down the steep canyon side
My feet on a boulder
The size of the RAV
We bought so you and Natalie
Would be safer 4-wheel driving
On your way on icy highways
To swim meets in the winter
Petal by red peony petal
I set your ashes free.

All the while sobbing Annie Annie
I love you
Being drowned out by the
Hard white pounding water
On even harder granite.
I never called you Annie
But now you have to hear me
I can't let go
Even of your little bag of ashes
I cry and clutch and beg
I can't go on
But I have to
Let go and go on.

There's frost on the grass
In Wild Horse this morning.
I love you Annie always.
Here among the grasses and the trees
You'll become part of
The life force of Wild Horse
My sweet baby
My beautiful innocent wife
Gone forever
But still here inside me
In my crying arms and bones.

Looking for the Village

January 18, 2006

When I came home from Paraguay
After two years in the Peace Corps
I was still looking for a way to help
So I earned a teaching certificate and
Applied to the Mackay Public Schools.

The only question I remember Palmer asking
At the interview was,
"Do you think you can live here?"

I thought I could, for four years,
Went through the 8.3 Mt. Borah earthquake in year two
And on Halloween of year three
A stranger came to town
To take care of his mother.

At the costume party he was dressed like
Charlie Chaplin with a hat and cane
While I was a drum majorette in falsies:
He thought I had boobs and
I thought he had hair.

What we learned about each other
In the ensuing twenty years
Filled my life until it ended
Two years ago on Mother's Day
When I was killed on my bicycle
Minding my own business
Obeying the law.

I left our daughter in his hands.
He took my ashes in his trembling hands
Back to Idaho to distribute them
As we saw fit.

Now I hear he's going out with other women.
We never talked about what he would do if I were gone.
We were both amateur statisticians who assumed
He would die first, being ten years older,
And the surviving spouse's problems would be mine.

He shouldn't have to iron out the ironies.
He has to live and take care of himself.
I miss my life and him
More than can be told.
In my dreams I'm always with him
On all saint's eve in Idaho
Each time like the first time
Filled with wonder, stars and love.

The Crumbs of Christmas

On Christmas morning discovering the crumbs
Of the cookies and the dab of milk
Natalie had set out by the fireplace for Santa Claus,
I went into the living room and saw the dollhouse
Ann had assembled and wrapped for her under the tree
And I moved on to the window and looked out
Into the still light of the coming day
With the haunting words of Thomas Paine in my head
And burst into tears.

I am responsible for children in a world about to unravel
And nothing I try to do about it seems to help.

Emily had already left thru the kitchen door
To tend to the Inglis' dogs while they're on vacation
And we exchange Merry Christmases
While I was still standing over the kitchen heat vent reading
Charles Beard's "Toward a Reconsideration of Democracy."

I can only make ourselves secure to a degree
Before the urge and the necessity to apply myself
To the larger problems of the rest of the people
Distracts me with its fatal urgency.

I spend most of my free time studying Japanese
For syntactical and process clues to a resilient perspective,
While at the same time tickled with twinges of nostalgia
For my student and childless days
When I was as free with apocalyptic advice as I wanted to be
Certain that the physical truth of all situations
Will settle them with or without human acquiescence or understanding.

Now the liberty of the child has been roped with the bonds of the parent
In Christmases past which I can barely recall
Yet those drunken epics still play on my retinas
With a careening cast of thousands
Skidding across the frozen deserts of Idaho
Amid the Catholic clatter of Puerto Vallarta.

I see a jogger out the window in my peripheral vision
And remember I was born to run
Away from responsibilities as soon as they present themselves
Whether those of poetry or parenting and yet I can't.

Chained to my desk, to bookkeeping, to wondering (if)
"Am I doing the right thing?"
Secure in our family's love
It is the certainties in the future and not the uncertainties
That bring on the child-like tears.

Turning the Mattress / by Myself

For Ann, September 17, 2004

Together we always laughed a lot
Turning our mattress and trying to remember
Which way we turned it last time.

This time it's my turn
To turn the mattress, by myself
Wash the sheets and kiss the sweaty
Pillow case of summer goodbye.

I've been sleeping so hard
I was making a hole in the bed,
An impression I could fall right through
To the long red stain on the other side.

My reluctance to accept the mess
Your death turned life into
Isn't helped by holding on
To this king size
"Bed of Roses" model.

When tears turn on I turn in
Early and alone
Missing love you freely shared
With no one to help me turn
Memories on the mattress
Into something better than
This rotisserie of pain.

Wild Horse as Winter Sets

December 17, 2004

Indifferent to the narrow
Passage of time against us
Five days from the axial earth tilt solstice
I'm reminded that you rode
Your dirt bike happily with friends
On that rough country road
As fresh as the air will ever be
Again in the sagebrush, pine and boulders
You're watching
As closely as anyone who's had
Their head torn off and scattered down the highway can
The rest of our tiny life
Come perilously apart.

Feet and Who They Fall for

For Annie, February 20, 2005

Pero no amo tus pies
sino porque anduvieron
sobre la tierra y sobre
el viento y sobre el agua
hasta que me encontraron
                    Neruda "Tus Pies"

You walked across the Andes and rafted
Down the Amazon to Manaus.

You walked out of South Dakota
To Pocatello and into
Mexico and Spain before you
Walked into Mackay responding to
The superintendent's question
"Do you think you can live here?"
Where one starlit night in time
We danced into each other other's arms.

Then we walked in Walla Walla
Up Karakuni Daki in Kyushu
Across the Sea of Japan in a beetle to Pusan
Down Playa de la Ropa in Zihautenejo
As far around Crater Lake as we could get in the snow
And last April at Puerto Peñasco.

You walked two years in Paraguay in
The Peace Corps
Twenty-two years walking the hallways of
Public education
Giving yourself back
To the system
And then, when you needed it,
The system walked out on you.

Cashing In Cashing Out

St. Patrick's Day, March 17, 2005

After ten months of tedious third-party hassle
The insurance companies finally shell out.

I could leave all the money on the counter
If I could have you back;
Walk out the door with you
Naked barefoot broke
Down the street together
Holding hands in love.

But you're gone forever
I'll be taking steps
With you inside me and
Our money on my back.

Happy Anniversary

For Ann, June 19, 2005

1.

Happy anniversary Ann.
My second without you.
You've been gone for a year and forty days.
I decided to cheer myself up by remembering
Ten beautiful things we did together.

First the wedding itself,
Planning it, discovering that there was only
One weekend available all summer
That wouldn't inconvenience either one of us
Or some significant member of the extended family.

How they all came
Don and Dee, My mom and dad
Our brothers and sisters
Molly couldn't come because she was pregnant with Camille.
My brother Don
Chloe as a babe in arms
Who just graduated from Arts and Science High School
In Durham, North Carolina.

How I broke the wedding up by blubbering my lines
Donna's voice cracked singing our song
"Bridge over Troubled Waters."
Emily and Johanna were flower girls
Judy played the hammer dulcimer.
The night before wedding dinner at Rees Mansion
When Adrian the cook's toupee slipped in the heat.

2.

Our beautiful wedding night at the honeymoon suite downtown
All our beautiful loving
From the first starfilled night in Mackay where we met on Halloween.
How I went back for Thanksgiving
Cooked you a chicken dinner while you worked
At Mackay's Public Schools.
You came to spend Christmas at our house
With me and Emily.
Our tryst in spring in Boise.
We went skiing up toward Idaho City.
You came to spend the summer
Before your six weeks in Mexico with
The Experiment in International Living
Trying to get drunken teenagers to get
Just a little grateful for the chance to learn something.
I wanted you to stay, not go to Idaho State for more degrees in speech pathology.
And you did even though I was terrified of your PMS.

3.

"You can't throw me away just because I have an illness," you said.
And in my bone marrow I agreed with this pre-wedding vow
In sickness and in health
Love will get us through.
But it took two years
One of which you lived at Palouse Palace down the street.
Because you spoke Spanish
Getting a job around here was relatively easy
Although the jobs themselves were not.
How hard you worked, how much you cared
About your students
Neither I nor they will ever forget.
Even Braullio a hard case, wrote a letter for you that
Chris Anderson showed me after you were killed.

4.

I don't know which one of our Mexican trips matters the most:
The first one to Puerto Vallarta where we got stung by a time share;
The second one to Zihuatenejo with all the beautiful beach
Where we left our camera on the table for some beach boy to steal;
Our last one to Puerto Peñasco and Rocky Point
Where we swam with the seals and walked to the waters edge;
Or the one we never took
Dreaming of going to Puerto Escondido together
Thinking maybe of retiring in Mexico
Or at least having a permanent place
We could go back to
Where it was warm and we didn't have to work
Where the food was good and the living was easy
Where some of what time we'd earned could have been spent
Gazing into one another's eyes.

5.

We were learning how to love one another,
How to living with the little irritating things
That break other marriages apart with contempt.
How many times the Nissan van let us down
With its insolvable electrical problems
And its revolutionary sliding doors.

6.

Maybe the biggest day of all was July 22, 1990,
The day Natalie was born and we walked
In the 100 plus degree heat in the sweltering garden
Just outside the maternity rooms at
General Hospital
And the nurse had you pushing even though
You were only halfway dilated
And nearly exhausted by the time Dr. Karmy
Rescued you from that bad advice.
Natalie was born just before midnight
On the Cancer/Leo cusp
And thirteen year old Emily was there to help
And our family was born.

7.
Who could forget
Our lost year in Japan
The typhoon Ju Yon Go in Achiokisan's house in Meinohama.
They wouldn't rent the new apartment to us
Because we were gaijin.
Climbing Karikuni Dake on Spring Vacation
How Natalie startled us both by saying
"I want to go everywhere and jump into the darkness."

8.
Coming back to Idaho for my mother's birthday party
The reunions with Stan and Joy, Marlene and Chuck,
My last terrible visit there on Memorial Day
To scatter your ashes in Wild Horse.
How you hated to go up the Lochsa
Preferring the longer route through Spokane.
The time of the forest fire, actually both times,
The first time we went past Shoup to Colson Crik,
The second last time we were down there for
The jet boat reunion to Barth Hotsprings over Salmon Falls.

9.
No report of our love would be complete without
The story of our firwood floors
Here in the McGilvarey Victorian
Where we discussed the problem for nearly twenty years:
Two rooms covered by wornout anso nylon maroon carpet
With cat odor that would not come out;
The other two rooms painted dark brown when we got here
And you later painted light brown while we argued the merits of
Carpet v. refinishing and the seasons turned into years melded into
Decades of disagreement before we took the plunge and
Made the beautiful straight grained fir floors shine
A few months before you were killed
The way they undoubtedly did when the house was new
100 years ago in 1905.

10.

That was the year my father was born
And your mother died when you were only nineteen
And Natalie was thirteen when you were killed
And today is Father's Day and I'm her father
And her mother now,
A house frau and frustrated
Father of a teenager.
I'm doing the best that I can is what I cry
Often into the night
Especially the night she didn't come home
But I welcomed her in the morning crying
You're always welcome here
Come back anytime
This is your home.

Wild Water

July 22, 2005

I can see why you liked to
Mountain bike in Wild Horse.
Last night I hiked 2.5 miles
Up to the mines.
This morning before breakfast
I drove a mile further,
Not quite white
Knuckle driving
To where old Hyndman towers
In the morning lite
Looking as you know
Like a mini-Matterhorn.

I go out onto the rocks
Where I let you go again
Still wailing at the insane
Unfairness of it all.
I aged ten years
The week you died.
Here the pounding undercurrent
Fractals the sound of water.
People ask me how I feel.
Will several hundred different ways an hour be enough?

Lonely September Moon

September 21, 2005

The moon appears
As it often does
The way it appeared
After Yoga
When we used to go
Together.

My best friend Edward died
The day after Christmas.
You were killed
On Mother's day.

There is a holiday for death
And it's the day we met:
Halloween.

It's hard to get rid of
The bitter taste
Why me
Giving death to twins?

Riding through the Night in a Shirt of Stars
December 9, 2005

Mars is low in the west.
Arcturus defines the dawn.
The bridge is thick with frost.
Orion stands over the river.
Tears were freezing to my face
18 months after your last ride.

I jumped two white tailed deer;
Saw a Great Blue Heron skim the lake.
I prefer the rippling lake
To the fractal undifferentiated auditory
Pounding of the water over the ripraps.

Ice puddles in the road ruts.
The trail is hard and lumpy in the springtime,
September it's full of finely powdered dust.
By the time I get to turning back
The visuals were down to
Mars hazed out in HAZMATS,
Sirius and Betelgeuse.

Soon I will descend into the lake's
Orange cottonwood necklace
Technicolor clouds reflecting on the surface.

Dawn swallowed Antares.
The invisible helicopter
Chops the wind.

The Hearth

Late yesterday afternoon, early evening after dinner,
For it was the longest day of the year,
The day between our tenth wedding anniversary and Father's Day,
The ten-year-old neighbor boy from the third house down
    Palouse Street
Rang the doorbell unannounced to pay us a visit.

In a moment he was romping on the floor
With Natalie and the mini-dachshund Penny,
As they raced from room to room, shrieking with pleasure
In a world almost of their own.

Ann admonished them to "Quit running through your dad's office.
Can't you see he's working in there?"
My office doors, open ten feet wide on both sides,
Make the office an integral part of the house.

I remonstrated that "No, it's ok if they run through my office."
It was Saturday and I was benefiting from the distraction.

Before long I noticed Christopher, feeling at home,
Sitting in the middle of the living room floor,
Taking off first his shoes and then his socks.

A warm light of pleasure filled my body and
The four wide rooms of their circular track,
As the children went on romping barefoot with even more abandon.

"That was very interesting," Natalie announced,
Hopping back up on the love seat
After Sue, his mother, came to call Chris home.

I come more and more to understand my purpose.
That he and they could feel so at home,
Safe and nonthreatened
Is what stokes my inner volcano.

This is what I'm good for.
This is what I'm good at.
This is what I'm supposed to have done:
To sacrifice everything to provide a hearth
To take what turns out to be
A supporting role
In the disappearing act of love.

Great Blue Heron on a Poplar Snag

June 18, 2005

Great Blue Heron lands on a poplar snag
Making me wonder momentarily
How a pterodactyl got all the way here
From the late Cretaceous

Until I realize this beautiful bird
Got here the same way the rest of us did:
One egg at a time.